READY, SE

THE 21-DAY
FAST START

A PROVEN BLUEPRINT FOR AWAKENING
YOUR FINANCIAL STEWARDSHIP

GEORGE B. THOMPSON
Edited by Thomas Z. Lukoma

The 21-Day Fast Start: A Proven Blueprint for Awakening Your Financial Stewardship

Copyright © 2023 George B. Thompson

ISBN: 9798373040532

ISBN 13: 979-8373040532 (Prosperity Publishing)

Prosperity Publishing, Los Angeles, CA

The purpose of this book is to educate. Many facts set forth in this publication were obtained from sources believed to be reliable but cannot be guaranteed with respect to accûracy. Any application of the investment or health advice herein is at the reader's own discretion and risk. If additional financial or health assistance is required, seek the advice of a financial or health professional. The author and the publisher shall have neither liability nor responsibility to any person or entity with respect to loss, damage, or injury caused or alleged to be caused directly or indirectly by the information contained in this book.

All scripture quotations, unless otherwise indicated, are taken from the Holy Bible, New International Version (NIV). Copyright 1973, 1978, 1984, 2011 by Biblica Inc. Used by permission of Zondervan. All rights reserved worldwide. www.zondervan.com. The "NIV" and "New International Version" are trademarks registered in the US Patent and Trademark Office by Biblica Inc.

Layout and design by: Ljiljana Pavkov

Printed in the United States of America

George Thompson is available as a keynote speaker at conventions, seminars, and workshops, as well as for organizations. If you would like to discuss a possible speaking engagement, send an e-mail to concierge@thompsonwm.com

For additional copies or bulk purchasing of this book, please contact Prosperity Publishing:

Prosperity Publishing
PO Box 90761
Los Angeles, CA 90009
(800) 452-8001

www.georgebthompson.com

CONTENTS

INTRODUCTION

I wrote this book to help you take control of your finances and transform your relationship with money in just 21 days. We live in a fast-paced world where it's easy to get caught up in the rat race of trying to "keep up with the Joneses" and constantly chasing more money.

But what if there was a way to break free from this cycle and achieve true financial freedom?

This book will guide you through a 21-day journey to help you understand your current financial situation, identify any limiting beliefs about money, and create a plan to achieve your financial goals. Whether you're struggling to make ends meet or want to take your finances to the next level, this book is for you.

In this book, I will cover the five levels of financial being: struggling, steady, solid, surplus, and service. I'll also delve into the power of your mindset and how your thoughts and beliefs about money can either hold you back or propel you forward. You'll learn practical budgeting, saving, and investing strategies, as well as tips for reducing debt and building wealth.

I designed the book to encourage you to take action by completing daily exercises and creating a personalized action plan. By the end of the 21 days, you will have a clear understanding of your financial situation, a plan to achieve your financial goals, and the knowledge and tools to maintain your financial freedom for the long term.

I understand that the subject of money can be overwhelming and often stressful. But with the right mindset and a practical plan, anyone can achieve financial freedom. So, let's begin this journey together and discover your true financial potential.

THE 21-DAY
FAST START

DAY 1

What is your level?

"The tongue has the power of life and death, and those who love it will eat its fruit."

(Proverbs 18:21)

Broke is a state of mind. How you think about and talk about your money determines your long-term financial well-being. Most of us have at least one source of income, but what you do with that income determines your financial level.

You must know where you stand financially, so I have a simple approach called the 5 Levels of Financial Being that helps you tell yourself the truth about your situation. And once you know the truth, you can implement the plan that fits your level.

The five levels are

1. **Struggling:** This is the inability to keep up with your financial obligations. Every month there is more month than money, and you get further behind as time passes.

2. **Steady:** At this level, you make just enough to pay your bills, but there is nothing left over for saving and investing. So if anything catastrophic happens to your income or expenses, you quickly fall back into the struggling level because you have nothing to bridge the gap.

3. **Solid:** You can "breathe" financially at this level. You have enough to pay your bills, take a non-debt-fueled vacation, put money in your retirement savings, and give charitable contributions. You have a good foundation for longer-term financial success.

   Warning: Some people believe they are at this level when, in reality, they are a 'strong steady.' To correctly determine if you are solid, you need to consider longer-term financial costs (like college savings) that should be in your monthly budget.

4. **Surplus:** At this level, you have extra money, over and above what you need to meet your financial priorities. You can ponder what happens with that extra money without harming your financial future.

5. **Service:** This is the highest level. At Service, the kind of thinking you do about money is primarily long-term and legacy-driven rather than immediate or medium-term goals.

Today, take some time to pinpoint which of these five levels is your actual situation. Regardless of which one you fall into, God can work with you when you are honest about your situation and ask for help.

Take ACTION

- Read this article about the 5 Levels of Financial Being:
  https://www.georgebthompson.com/financial-level

- Take the Financial Levels Quiz here:
  https://www.georgebthompson.com/my-level/

DAY 2

Develop your M.I.N.D.

*"The simple believe anything,
but the prudent give thought to their steps."*

(Proverbs 14:15)

You must develop your mind.

I am not referring to going back to school or taking an online course. When it comes to your financial success, you need to develop the following four areas: **M**oney, **I**ntelligence, **N**eed, and **D**iscipline.

Money is just an object, and it has no morals or feelings. The way you use it determines your level of financial success. As you develop your ability to manage money, your financial situation improves.

Intelligence refers to your money intelligence. Just as emotional intelligence determines how successful you are in your relationships, money intelligence determines how well you make money-related decisions – how "money smart" you are.

Need is related to how badly you want to be a good steward of your finances – your desire to be successful in this area. With this desire, you will take the necessary actions to get your results and do the hard work.

Discipline is the cornerstone for turning an idea into reality. With your financial stewardship, you must commit to making a change and stick with it regardless of how you feel. "Do the do" because it is the only way to change things around.

Today, evaluate yourself in these four areas and identify where you are weak and where you are strong.

Write this down in your journal.

Take ACTION

- Write in your journal about your mindset in MIND areas. Answer the following questions in the journal:
  o What does money mean to you?
  o How 'smart' are you with money? Who do you know that is 'smart' with their finances?
  o How strong is your desire to be a better steward of your money? What stands in the way of you making progress toward this goal?
  o What simple change can you make today to be more disciplined with your money?

DAY 3

Who owns what you have?

"The earth is the LORD's, and everything in it,
the world, and all who live in it; for he founded it
on the seas and established it on the waters."

(Psalm 24:1-2)

How often do you use the word "mine" or some version of it during the day?

"My" stuff, "my" money, "our" home – the list is endless. It's easy to believe that you own the things you have when God's word tells us a very different story.

Everything on the earth is the Lord's – He owns it all, and we do not own anything. This truth goes back to the Garden of Eden when God gave Adam the job of caring for His creation. We have always had the assignment of caretakers – stewards – not owners. God has entrusted us with the things we have, but His purposes ultimately need to be achieved through those things.

When you truly understand this, your attitude towards your money changes because you realize that correctly managing every penny in your possession is an act of worship – an act of love and obedience towards your heavenly Father.

True financial prosperity comes from changing your lens and seeing money the way God sees it.

Here are some steps to incorporate into your 21-Day Fast Start that will help you with that goal:

- Only buy what you NEED.

- Use all cash for purchases for a whole week. Only use credit or debit cards if you have no other option, as in a self-pay parking garage or gas at Costco. Doing so will help you be more intentional about how you use money.

- No eating out. Only purchase what you need for breakfast, lunch, dinner, and any modest snacks for the next 21 days at the grocery store.

- Only buy necessary items. No chips, no movie tickets, and no shoes, even if they are on clearance, unless you don't have any to wear.

- Think about the items you purchase throughout the Fast Start and decide if they are a want, need, or wish.

Take ACTION

- Read about the 5 reasons you may miss the mark with stewardship here: *https://www.georgebthompson.com/ life-stewardship-5-reasons*

DAY 4 **Your true story**

"A good person leaves an inheritance for their children's children, but a sinner's wealth is stored up for the righteous."

(Proverbs 13:22)

Your ability to be honest with yourself is one of your greatest assets – especially regarding your finances. Avoiding the truth does not change it – it only brings you more anxiety.

In your financial stewardship: "Your spending history IS your true story." Suppose you say purchasing a new home is your highest priority, and your bank transactions include a large portion of your income going to expensive trips to Caribbean islands. In that case, your actual story is likely that travel is more important to you than your stated long-term home purchase goal.

Prioritizing travel is fine (if you have the money for it) – just be honest with yourself that this is your priority before you get frustrated that you are not reaching your down payment saving goal!

Today, take the time to analyze your true story by reviewing your last three months of transactions in all your bank accounts and credit card statements. Choose simple categories for your spending based on how you live. And then, add the totals in each category to see the full amounts.

If you have time, write the letters S, L, or O next to each spending category. The letters stand for

- **Spend it:** this is all the categories where you buy things that don't go up in value.

- **Lend it:** this is any category where you buy or save for something you will then lend out for a return.

- **Own something:** Refers to any purchase or savings for an item that will grow in value.

Take ACTION

- Without any judgment of yourself, write down your three TRUE priorities in your journal based on your spending history.

DAY 5 | **The stages of financial growth**

"Suppose one of you wants to build a tower. Won't you first sit down and estimate the cost to see if you have enough money to complete it?"

(Luke 14:28)

Yesterday we spoke about the five levels of financial being. You had a chance to evaluate which group best described your situation. The purpose of that exercise is to develop a plan that is most relevant to your situation.

If you are Struggling, the goal is to get to Steady – if you are Steady, the goal is to get you to Solid and so on, until you achieve Service.

Service may seem far away, but it is achievable over time.

Four stages of financial growth help you to navigate this journey. They help to give you specific actions and goals that will build on each other to make you more successful.

The steps are sequential, so if you work on them in order, you increase your chances of success.

1. **Spending Control** – Controlling how you spend money is the most fundamental skill in wealth building. It is the first step in effectively managing the funds that you already have. Before you can work on any other actions, you need positive cash flow – which comes from having some money left over after you have paid for all your expenses.

2. **Debt Elimination** – trying to build wealth while still in debt is a losing plan because you always allocate a portion of your cash flow to somebody else's agenda. That's why I focus so much on helping you master this step.

3. **SaVesting** – this is the combination of Saving and Investing. You don't have to build up a vast savings fund before it is okay for you to invest because doing so makes you miss out on one of the essential elements of investing: time.

4. **Building Your Wealth Machine** – once you have the first three stages under control, this is the most fun part – putting your money to work in suitable vehicles.

If you are Struggling, you should start with Spending Control and Debt Elimination. To go from Steady to Solid, aggressively focus on Debt Elimination and SaVesting. To move from Solid to Surplus, dig deep into SaVesting and start building your Wealth Machine.

Take ACTION

- Read this article for a practical example of how getting started on the four stages of financial growth might look: *https://www.georgebthompson.com/ getting-started-on-the-four-stages-of-financial-growth*

DAY 6

The Wealth Cycle

*"And God is able to bless you abundantly,
so that in all things at all times,
having all that you need,
you will abound in every good work."*

2 Corinthians 9:8

Becoming wealthy is not the result of a single event; winning the lottery only makes you rich if you have the wisdom to take care of the money and manage it properly. Instead, wealth building consists of four steps repeated in a cycle regardless of your net worth.

These four steps are what I call The Wealth Cycle, and mastering them when you have modest means will set you up for when you start moving up the five levels.

The core element of the four steps is your cash flow, the difference between how much money you bring in and how much goes out. Each step is an action that you must do with your cash flow.

Step One: Monitor Your Cashflow

Monitoring cash flow is the art of answering the question: "where does your money go?" The better you can answer that question, the more control you will feel over your finances – even when trying to move from Struggling to Steady.

Step Two: Analyze Your Cashflow

Change is only possible if you know what actions to take and what steps to take. You need to understand where your problems reside. When you analyze your cash flow, you divide your spending into three categories: Installment Debt, Budget, and Prosperity Dollars.[1] The goal is to get as much of your cash flow as possible into Prosperity Dollars.

Step Three: Increase Your Cashflow

There are only two ways to increase your cash flow: lower your expenses or increase your income.

Increasing your cash flow is the only way to make more money into Prosperity Dollars.

Step Four: Distribute Your Cashflow

Once you complete the first three steps and have created a surplus of money, you must distribute that surplus into suitable vehicles. This distribution decides what portion of your money goes into investments, real estate, and business ventures.

---

[1] Prosperity Dollars – money in your budget that goes towards improving your long-term financial health (e.g. giving tithes or depositing into your 401K).

When you reach step four, go back to step one and repeat the process.

Look at the last five days of your Spending Journal. Do you see any areas in which you can improve?

Take ACTION

- If you want to go more in-depth with The Wealth Cycle, I wrote a book about it that you can purchase here: *https://www.amazon.com/Wealth-Cycle -Building-Financial-Legacy/ dp/0967485827*

DAY 7

Getting your spending under control

"Be sure you know the condition of your flocks, give careful attention to your herds; for riches do not endure forever, and a crown is not secure for all generations."

(Proverbs 27:23-24)

B y now, you should be more aware of how you spend your money. You don't need to know where every penny has gone, but you should have a general idea of the critical areas you must consider adjusting. It's time to take action to control any areas you are not managing as well as you can.

The best way to do this is to use a budget.

Okay, I know for many people, the "b-word" brings up all sorts of emotions like feeling "controlled" or "trapped." Or it might be that you are worried that you could never be disciplined enough to manage your money with a budget.

I would like you to change the way you think about your budget. Rather than an authoritarian ruler over your life, your budget is your playbook.

Any coach in a team sport knows that going into a game without a game plan is a grave mistake. Coaches use playbooks to explain their approaches and strategies to defeat opponents. Keeping the playbook in their head doesn't work because our minds can change things and give us false information. In the heat of a game, coaches need the playbook to communicate with their team what they need to do.

In your financial life, the coach is you, the players are your money, and the playbook is your budget. You use your playbook to tell your players what to do so that they can win.

Today, create an outline of your money playbook for a few minutes, and write out your needs, wants, and wishes. Divide your spending categories into these three groups and add a dollar amount to each category. This breakdown should represent what you believe is the monthly need for the category.

Next, add all your monthly income sources and compare that number to the total spending you planned. If your income is less than the playbook's spending plan, you now have a clear understanding of how to prioritize what you fund first (hint hint – your needs) – and what you can do without (hint hint – your wants and wishes).

Take ACTION

- Go to this link for a video with a helpful way to think about the job your budget plays in your money life: *https://www.youtube.com/watch?v =bDVJN95yFJc*

DAY 8

Stop Spending Into Debt

"The rich rule over the poor, and the borrower is slave to the lender."

Proverbs 22:7

Yesterday, when you created your money playbook (your budget), there was one category of expenses that is the most damaging to your Wealth Cycle if you are Struggling, Steady or Solid – debt.

In my book, *The Wealth Cycle*, I refer to debt to credit cards as "plastic crack" – the use of credit cards leaves you with an artificial high, and when you come down and get the bill, reality sets in. At that point, the high is long gone. But you still owe the original amount you spent plus interest.

You are making someone else rich from the sweat of your brow.

In the book, I provide four rules for getting out of debt:

- **Stop spending** – be disciplined about the money playbook you set up and stick to your plan

- **Pay the minimum** on all cards except one.

- **Establish a debt multiplier of $100** minimum and apply it as an addition to the monthly payment of your smallest debt. I describe this process in detail in the book.

- **Stay disciplined** – there will be times when you want to give up, but keep your eyes on the final destination: Surplus.

Your steady focus on eliminating your debt will start to pick up steam as you pay off the balances of each debt. It may seem slow-moving at first, but the momentum will pick up if you stick with it, and before you know it, your playbook will point more toward wealth-building than debt bills.

Today, take a moment to figure out how to adjust your money playbook so that you have at least $100 per month to put toward your debt multiplier; if you can find more than $100, even better.

Take ACTION

- Read this article about Debt Slavery:
  https://www.georgebthompson.com/debt -slavery-is-tied-to-your-financial-struggle

DAY 9

Do G.O.O.D. ...
Get out of debt!

"Let no debt remain outstanding,
except the continuing debt to love one another,
for whoever loves has fulfilled the law."

(Romans 13:8)

Yesterday, I gave you a practical understanding of how to get out of debt. Today, we'll use an example to see how you can take action on what you learned. There are three critical steps to making the Debt Eliminator work for you:

- List all of your debts

- Decide on the size of your Debt Multiplier

- Turn the Debt Multiplier into a Debt ELIMINATOR

Step 1: List all of your debts

Take a complete inventory of your debts by listing them from smallest to most significant using the Debt Eliminator table below. Include every creditor, the monthly payment, the outstanding balance, and the interest rate. Here is an example with it all filled out:

Debt	Min. monthly payment	Balance	Interest rate	Debt Eliminator	Priority	Time
Dept. store card #1	$15	$275	18%			
Dept. store card #2	$25	$500	18%			
Dept. store card #3	$40	$1,200	18%			
Major credit card #1	$45	$1,500	18%			
Major credit card #2	$90	$3,000	18%			
Major credit card #3	$125	$4,200	18%			
Car loan	$275	$11,000	12%			
Student loan	$250	$20,000	6%			
Mortgage	$1,000	$150,000	7%			
Total	$1,865	$191,675				

Step 2: Decide the size of your debt multiplier

Based on your budget, find at least $100 that you can afford to apply consistently monthly to your debt. That amount should be over and above what you pay on your debt. The larger you can make this amount, the faster you will pay off your debt.

Step 3: Turn your debt multiplier into a debt ELIMINATOR

Continue paying the minimum payment on all cards except the smallest balance. For that card, pay the minimum plus $100. Doing so makes your payoff faster. When you have paid off the first debt, apply the $100 plus the amount you were paying to the first debt to the next smallest debt.

Here is an illustration of how this might look and how long it would take to pay off all the debt:

Debt	Min. monthly payment	Balance	Interest rate	Debt Eliminator	Priority	Time (months)
Dept. store card #1	$15	$275	18%	$115	1	3
Dept. store card #2	$25	$500	18%	$140	2	6
Dept. store card #3	$40	$1,200	18%	$180	3	12
Major credit card #1	$45	$1,500	18%	$225	4	18
Major credit card #2	$90	$3,000	18%	$315	5	25
Major credit card #3	$125	$4,200	18%	$440	6	31
Car loan	$275	$11,000	12%	$715	7	38
Student loan	$250	$20,000	6%	$965	8	53
Mortgage	$1,000	$150,000	7%	$1,965	9	147
Total	**$1,865**	**$191,675**				**147**

Continue the debt multiplier process until you have paid off all the debts.

There are two essential requirements to ensure this process works:

- Make sure to keep up with ALL the minimum payments on the other debts you still need to eliminate.

- Do NOT (and this is the most important thing) incur any additional debt.

Take ACTION

- Listen to these two podcast episodes on *How to Get out of Debt*

  - Part 1:
    https://anchor.fm/set-4-life/episodes/How-to-get-out-of-debt-pt--1-eido2p

  - Part 2:
    https://anchor.fm/set-4-life/episodes/How-to-get-out-of-debt-pt--2-ej5fni

- If you have my book, *The Wealth Cycle*, you can read about this debt multiplier process in detail in the *Debt Elimination* chapter.

DAY 10

Humble yourself

*"Pride brings a person low,
but the lowly in spirit gain honor."*

(Proverbs 29:23)

L et's detour from our regular programming today and talk about pride.

Confidence and pride are often confused, especially in a country like the United States, where people view 'self-made wealth' as a worthy aspiration for everyone. There is a heightened focus on your internal 'power' and how you can change things around you just by becoming better or more skilled at getting things done.

This approach to life becomes dangerous if you leave God out of the picture because when you experience financial success, you become prideful about your capabilities instead of understanding that the money is for a purpose and not just a scorecard of your greatness. You can also begin to look down on other people that are not

as financially successful as you because you view their 'lower' financial status as a character flaw.

The best way to keep things in perspective as you grow in your financial journey is to be humbly confident. Derive your sense of accomplishment and confidence in your financial abilities from understanding the greater purpose of stewardship that God has given you. You are the conduit to somebody else's blessing, and as you show yourself faithful with the resources that God has put in your hand, He can trust you to align those resources with the grand vision He has for His creation.

Take ACTION

- Identify somebody in your community who is struggling and find a way to bless them in a small way. Keep the deed to yourself and your inner circle - you are not doing this for the accolades about your kindness, and you are doing it to be an extension of God's grace towards them.

DAY 11

You are a SaVestor

> *"His master replied, 'You wicked, lazy servant!*
> *So, you knew that I harvest where I have not sown*
> *and gather where I have not scattered seed?*
> *Well then, you should have put my money on*
> *deposit with the bankers, so that when I returned*
> *I would have received it back with interest."*
>
> (Matthew 25:26-27)

You now have a clear strategy in place. You have created your money playbook (budget) to ensure you are playing the money game to win. And you have put your debt eliminator in place to accelerate your escape from debt bondage.

Congratulations, you are making things happen and working your way up the five levels of financial being.

Budgeting and debt elimination are about playing defense with your money – now it's time to put some offense into place with saving – the process of setting aside some of your current cash flow for future use. It is

a critical part of your wealth cycle because it creates your future "bench strength" to deal with life's unexpected twists and turns and take advantage of critical financial opportunities that you will encounter.

If you are Struggling or Steady, focus on these three steps first:

1. Save at least $1,000 to deal with any unexpected expenses that could throw your progress off
2. Stay consistent with your Debt Eliminator
3. Start contributing to your retirement savings vehicle (401k, IRA, etc.)

If you are Solid and still have debt, focus on these steps:

1. Increase your debt eliminator to more than $100, so you can pay the debt off faster
2. Contribute at least 1% of your income to your retirement savings
3. Start contributing to a mutual fund

If you are Surplus or Service, saving is driven by your entrepreneurial and contribution vision so that it will be more customized. You should still maintain the discipline of saving so that your stewardship stays intact.

Take ACTION

- Pick at least one of the suggested actions for your financial level and do one thing today that will get you started toward it.

DAY 12

Open your eyes

The wise store up choice food and olive oil,
but fools gulp theirs down."

(Proverbs 21:20)

What is your image of an investor? Do you think an investor is somebody on Wall Street wearing an expensive suit and barking orders at other people to buy and sell stocks? Does an investor look like somebody you don't see in the mirror?

If so, I will let you know a little secret today. Investors come in all shapes and sizes; you don't have to look a particular way or dress in a specific style to take advantage of the power of investing.

You just need to have some money, a plan, and some discipline.

Along with those three things, you need to develop what I call "new eyes." Develop a new way of looking at investments in the market and spotting new opportunities. The best way to do this is to walk through your

Day 12 • Open your eyes

day mentally and think about each of the products and services you have used since you woke up.

Think about when your alarm went off and which company made that electronic device or smartphone.

Then think about which department store you bought the sheets for your bed from.

Which company made the toothpaste you brushed your teeth with after you got out of bed? – and who made the soap you used for your shower?

As you continue this process, you will realize that before you even get to work, you will have interacted with dozens of companies that are good candidates for you to examine as potential investments.

Take ACTION

- Today, take a moment to do the exercise I just described; jot down ten to fifteen company names and start researching them. See which have these three characteristics: great products and services, excellent management, and intrinsic value.

- If you have my book, *The Wealth Cycle*, you can do this process in detail. Read the chapter called "SaVesting" (in the "Introduction to Investing" section), where I explain in more detail how to determine the characteristics of a good stock.

DAY 13

When you are old, you can still live well

*"A faithful person will be richly blessed,
but one eager to get rich will not go unpunished."*

(Proverbs 28:20)

N ot everyone has to think about funding a college education – but everyone has to think about how to pay for retirement. Unlike a college education, you cannot borrow money for retirement. So it is crucial to have a savings/investment plan for this area of your finances as early as possible.

There are five keys to retiring comfortably:

Key #1: Start Right Away

The most important thing to do regarding retirement investment (even if you are close to retirement) is to start. If you don't take action, you will not get an outcome.

Key #2: Use Tools from the Government

Take advantage of whichever government-qualified plan you are eligible to use. The plan could be a 401(k), 403(b), or IRA. If you are self-employed, you can take advantage of a SEP program. Each program has tax advantages that help you make the most of your savings.

Key #3: Make it Automatic

Don't leave your retirement savings up to your monthly financial whims.

Set up your plan, set up consistent, automatic payments into that plan – and then leave it alone. Have the funds automatically deducted from your paycheck, so you don't even see the funds.

Key #4: Start Collecting Eggs

Think of retirement investing as collecting eggs and putting them into baskets. You don't want to eat the eggs before they hatch; instead, you want to allow them to grow and hatch into whole chickens, which will, in turn, be able to lay more eggs and multiply your collection.

Key #5: Learn to Diversify

As your investments accumulate over time for your retirement, ensure you are not putting all your eggs in one basket. Diversifying where you put your assets is vital to protect you from changes in the market. Your portfolio should 'counterbalance' itself – when one part is down, another portion goes up.

Take ACTION

- By reading this article, educate yourself today about IRAs and consider opening one even if you already have another retirement plan:
https://www.georgebthompson.com/ira-saving-for-retirement-outside-of-work

DAY 14

Build an All-Star team

*"Two are better than one because
they have a good return for their labor:
If either one of them falls down, one can
help the other up. But pity anyone
who falls and has no one to help them up."*

Ecclesiastes 4:9-10

In this 21-Day Fast Start, I have referred to wealth building a lot, and this might make you uncomfortable because you associate riches with corruption or immorality. It's important to realize that money is merely a magnifier of character – it is not the money that determines whether you are good or bad. It is your character, and the money just magnifies the impact of who you are.

Suppose you understand this concept and the importance of stewardship. In that case, you realize that part of good stewardship is maximizing every opportunity that God presents to you, even when those opportunities are ways for you to build wealth.

So, if you are going to be the best steward of the possibilities before you, you must surround yourself with the right financial team. Regardless of how great a player on a team sport plays, they can only play some of the positions on the court or field. For that player's greatness to shine, they depend on a team that will help them cover all facets of the game.

If you plan to win in your finances, your team should consist of all-star players in the following roles:

- **Financial Advisor** – this person is like your financial team's quarterback or point guard. When this person is good, they see the whole picture and guide you in ways to use the rest of your team that maximize your success. Sometimes, they go by different names, like financial planners, financial consultants, or stockbrokers. The key here is that they should not be somebody making a commission on investments they sell to you, and their fee should be for giving you advice.

- **Accountant** – Taxes will always be one of your most significant expenses. A solid tax management plan is crucial to your financial success, and this is the principal value that an accountant provides.

- **Estate Lawyer** – If you plan to build a financial legacy, the lawyer you should always have on your financial team is an estate lawyer. They help you put a plan in place for when you eventually die. This plan is essential if you have a spouse or children.

- **Other Lawyers** – Depending on the nature of your wealth-building plan, you may also need to retain the services of a business lawyer and a real estate lawyer. Law is a specialized field, and it is a mistake

to try and cover all your legal 'bases' with one lawyer acting as a 'generalist.'

- **Other Professionals** – If you are investing in Real Estate, you will also want to have the following mem-
bers on your team: Real Estate Agent, Contractor,
Handyman, and Inspector

Take ACTION

- Today, take note of who is already on
your financial team, and if you are already
getting good service from them, there is no
need to change. If you still need to include
a critical member of the team, start looking
for referrals so that you can fill in the gaps.

- If you have my book, *The Wealth Cycle*,
you can find a more detailed look at
how to build your financial team by
reading the chapter on "Building Your
Wealth Machine."

DAY 15

You and your wealth machine

> *"Suppose one of you wants to build a tower. Won't you first sit down and estimate the cost to see if you have enough money to complete it? For if you lay the foundation and are not able to finish it, everyone who sees it will ridicule you, saying, "This person began to build and wasn't able to finish."*
>
> (Luke 14:28-30)

Yesterday we discussed the importance of building an all-star wealth-building team. As you work with this team, you will move through the foundational strategies for saving and investing. Once you have mastered those and generated surplus income, you can begin using more advanced wealth-building game plans.

Working through these strategies is what I call 'building your wealth machine' – aligning each of your income-producing assets and activities so that they work together to multiply your efforts.

There are three essential concepts to always keep in mind with your wealth machine:

- Diversify Your Portfolio
- Manage Your Buckets
- Manage Your Risk

Diversify Your Portfolio

As you develop more financial resources and have more options for where to put your money, you must create a framework that helps you to evaluate your entire portfolio. Ensure that you include a strategic mix of stocks, bonds, alternative investments, and real estate to maximize your effectiveness.

Manage Your Buckets

You should also manage the 'buckets' that catch your income – the jobs you give to your accumulated assets. A meaningful way to look at this concept is with consumption, contingency, and custodial categories. The consumption bucket is for assets you need to live on, spend or enjoy life, and the contingency bucket is for emergencies or 'just in case.' And the custodial bucket is for assets that are not needed in your life and will pass on to your surviving family when you die.

One mistake I see often is people failing to pay more attention to the contingency and custodial buckets because their consumption lifestyle is so high. So, they weaken their financial legacy or wipe it out if they have a crisis or pass away.

Manage Your Risk

Risk is inevitable when investing, and how you respond to it determines your outcomes. Ignoring and avoiding risk works against your wealth-building plans and eventually hinders your wealth machine. Learn how to manage and transfer risk to be successful.

Take ACTION

- For a closer look at your wealth machine, read the chapter on "Building Your Wealth Machine" in *The Wealth Cycle*.

DAY 16

You, the real estate investor

*"The highest heavens belong to the LORD,
but the earth he has given to mankind."*

(Psalm 115:16)

Real estate is a critical component of any comprehensive wealth-building plan. Three attributes are desirable about this type of investment:

- **Intrinsic value.** No two properties are the same, and a limited amount of land is available in any given geographical area. This finite nature of real estate means you can seek out places that are 'up-and-coming' and buy property at a value price, and once the area becomes more popular, the value of the property increases.

- **Proactive value creation.** You can proactively increase the value of your property by making improvements through renovations and landscaping.

- **Income-generating.** Properties you purchase to rent out can increase in value over time and provide you with a steady income when the tenants pay.

You might be thinking: "Wow, if real estate is so great, why isn't everybody doing it?".

Along with the benefits of real estate come risks and responsibilities that you must manage well to be successful. The best way to mitigate the risks of owning property is to have a strong team of professionals in your group.

Real estate agents help you understand local geographic markets.

Contractors and inspectors can help you evaluate the potential for expensive issues before you purchase the property.

And real estate lawyers help you to protect yourself as much as possible with the law – especially when you are buying and managing investment properties.

The first place to start with real estate investing is to purchase your primary residence the right way.

Take ACTION

- Read this article for more information on how to do so – Three elements to buying residential real estate right:
  https://www.georgebthompson.com/3-elements-to-buying-real-estate-right

DAY 17

Mind your business

"Each of you should use whatever gift you have received to serve others, as faithful stewards of God's grace in its various forms."

(1 Peter 4:10)

You may have never thought of it this way, but business is a form of service when motivated by the right spirit and focus. Maintain the mindset of a servant and instill that into the culture of your business if you want continued success as a business owner.

If you are considering starting a new business or taking over an existing one, I commend you for your vision. Business ownership is a great way to build a financial legacy – but it is also a great way to lose one. So, you must go into your venture with realistic expectations and a proper understanding of why you are doing it.

I use the Five P's as a shorthand for describing the different reasons people start businesses:

- **Passion** – you are incredibly passionate about an issue, and you see yourself running a business where you get to be around your passion all day. An example of this is somebody who loves cooking and opens a restaurant.

- **Personal Skill** – you are especially good at a specific skill, and you believe people will be willing to pay a premium for your skills. For example, a graphic designer who works for an agency decides to go solo and get their own gigs, eventually building a team around this into a business.

- **Product or Service** – you have an idea for a product or business that you believe has a market and want to build a business around it.

- **Profit** – you want to create value in the marketplace that will translate into profit. People with this motivation are not necessarily tied to one area or topic but are constantly looking for opportunities to uncover underserved markets.

- **Philosophy** – you want to change the world in a particular way with your business. The business acts as a for-profit enterprise and an opportunity to further a cause or a movement.

Consider which of these five motivations is driving you when looking at a business opportunity. The sweet spot for starting a business is checking off all five.

Take ACTION

- Read the "Business Strategy" section in *The Wealth Cycle* to get a comprehensive view of how to set yourself up for business success.

DAY 18

Do business right

"Better a little with the fear of the Lord,
than great wealth with turmoil."

(Proverbs 15:16).

I f you currently have a business or desire to build one in the future, it's crucial to understand how to balance hard work with wisdom in allocating your efforts. If you don't, you will always feel like your business is chaotic and overwhelming.

Our culture is currently obsessed with 'the grind' and 'hustling' as indicators that you are doing all that it takes to make a business successful - but you also need to have the wisdom to know when this crosses over into 'workaholism' and 'toxic productivity.' One of the ways to safeguard yourself from this trap is to allocate time to developing a clear strategy for your business and seeking input from trusted advisors to help you refine it.

I recommend keeping your plan simple by focusing on four pillars of your business:

- **New products and services** – if you are just starting your business, by default, your product or service is new. Once your product or service has been in the market for a while, you must develop a strategic approach to periodically rolling out new things. Otherwise, your business will grow stagnant and start to shrink.

- **Marketing** – people need to know about what you are selling, so it's essential to have a system for consistently sharing the benefits and features of your offering with your most likely buyers.

- **Operations** – you need a documented system for doing everything in your business. As your business grows, this will help you delegate tasks instead of being the only person who can do everything; your operations and how you design them are critical to ensuring that you consistently deliver quality to your customers or clients.

- **Reporting** – you need a system for knowing exactly how you are doing at any time with the business. Develop a business and financial dashboard that shows you all of the critical numbers for your business so that you can keep yourself and your team accountable and make decisions based on facts.

Take ACTION

- If you own a business or are planning to launch one, take some time to write down your business strategy using the four pillars outlined in today's lesson.

DAY 19

Yours and their money

*"So, they are no longer two, but one flesh.
Therefore, what God has joined together,
let no one separate."*

(Matthew 19:6)

To win financially as a couple, how you work together with money is critical. When you are single, personal finance only involves one decision-maker, whereas marriage is a partnership that requires cooperation.

There are ten areas I have observed that help couples operate in unity and succeed financially. I will share four of them with you today, and you can find the other six in the chapter on "Your Marriage and Your Money" in *The Wealth Cycle*.

If you are not married but plan to be one day, bookmark this page for future reference. And share it with friends and family who are married.

#1: Mine, Yours, Ours, or HIS

When you come together, your vocabulary around money must change. You are used to referring to 'my money,' 'my bank account,' 'your debt,' and 'your bills' – descriptions that imply that your financial lives are still separate. Start using 'ours' around everything financial. You are on this journey together.

Along with mastering the 'ours' of your finances, it's even more critical that the two of you are on the same page – that you are merely stewards of His money – God is the owner of everything you have.

#2: Giving as a Priority

If the two of you are not in agreement about your priorities as givers, you are setting yourselves up for long-term conflict that is impossible to resolve. You must have the same beliefs about tithing on your income and giving out of your overflow in charity.

#3: Operate on a Family Budget

Make sure you can see a consolidated view of the entire budget across your finances. Even if you have multiple accounts, you should never hide any aspects of your financial life from each other. Use a joint budget to ensure you align your priorities for how you spend the household income.

#4: Have Team Goals

Write your family vision together and make sure it covers the desires and aspirations of both of you. People who don't write down their goals have a meager chance of achieving them. And if you want to unite as a couple, it's vital to use written goals to ensure that the two of you are moving in the same direction rather than striving for different and sometimes opposing things.

Today, if you are married, have a conversation with your spouse about these four points and jointly evaluate how well you are doing. Make a plan for improvement if there are any significant gaps.

Take ACTION

- Schedule a 'game planning' date with your special someone and spend some time sharing your biggest dreams and aspirations at the moment – don't worry too much yet about how you will get to them – just focus on sharing

- Make sure to write all of the dreams and aspirations down and put a date in the calendar for one month later to review everything you wrote down; during that month, research the amount of money each dream and aspiration will require

- When you have that game planning date a month later, make three prioritized lists:

  1. A combined list of your shared goals
  2. A list of your special someone's goals
  3. A list of your goals

DAY 20

Financial intimacy with your partner

"Do not judge, and you will not be judged.
Do not condemn, and you will not be condemned.
Forgive and you will be forgiven."

(Luke 6:37)

Managing your finances well as an individual is already challenging for most people, so when you add another person's emotions, habits, wants, wishes, and desires into the mix, the complexity increases exponentially.

In my years of working with couples that struggle in this area, I have observed that they have usually chosen (or grown into) one of the following negative patterns when dealing with their money.

Day 20 • Financial intimacy with your partner

The Money Tyrant

The "money tyrant" pattern happens in one of two situations:

1. One spouse earns significantly more than the other
2. One spouse is a considerably better money manager than the other

When either of those things is true, there is a temptation to control everything to do with money without your partner's input. In these cases, the spouse in the power position often thinks they are doing the right thing by completely taking things over.

The Money Parent

The "money parent" pattern is a subset of the "money tyrant." However, the "money parent" is usually driven more by a need to nurture than control. In these situations, one partner sees it as their duty to educate the other partner about the right way to deal with money.

The Money Strangers

"Money strangers" in a marriage resist negotiating and compromising and have an unspoken lack of trust in each other. They manage their money separately from each other. In extreme cases, one or both of you have 'secret' bank accounts. And you hide financially significant information from each other.

If you exhibit any of the patterns I have outlined, you don't only have money problems in your marriage – you are eroding your ability to grow together intimately. Each way displays a lack of trust or an inability to treat the other spouse as an equal partner.

In a financially successful marriage, there are no "money tyrants," "money parents," or "money strangers." Both spouses respect each other's role in their financial future enough to work together as a team, and they create intimacy around their finances. That might seem like a strange word to use with money, but it's crucial to grasp this concept: *your relationship with money is highly emotional*. Therefore, it is impossible to separate your money patterns from the health of your relationship. Trying to do so moves you further away from each other instead of bringing you closer.

Take ACTION

- Take an honest look at your relationship and determine if you have any of the three dysfunctional relationship patterns around money.

- If you identify that you have one or more of the behaviors in your relationship, seek professional relationship counseling to help both of you develop a healthier way to relate.

DAY 21

What is your legacy?

"A good person leaves an inheritance for their children's children, but a sinner's wealth is stored up for the righteous."

(Proverbs 13:22)

When you think about your purpose in the world, how many generations do you think you will impact? The Bible expects us to leave an inheritance – a legacy – not just for our children but for our grandchildren. Doing so requires foresight and planning, and you can start that process today.

Although the word 'inheritance' invokes a discussion about generational wealth, whatever you pass down financially will be short-lived if you don't couple it with wisdom and knowledge. So when you think about 'Generational Wealth', consider these three components:

- **Knowledge** – provide your family tree with a 'short-cut' to their paths to success by teaching them the lessons

you learn in your lifetime, rather than leaving them to make the same mistakes you made; or miss opportunities that you were able to recognize and maximize

- **Tradition / Culture** – do you have traditions that your family has passed down from generation to generation? Find ways to document these traditions. And put systems (e.g., family reunions, digital family tree) into place so they can live on even after you are gone.

- **Finances** – organize your finances to maximize what will pass on to your family (without any drama) after you are gone.

On a more practical level, here are some key things to include in your generational wealth plan:

1. Income plan
2. Debt plan (Do G.O.O.D plan)
3. Investment plan (a) stocks, bonds, mutual funds (b) real estate
4. Taxes – make taxes efficient (don't pay too much) / Insurance – protect your assets (annuities, long-term care, life insurance)
5. Estate Planning – living trust, will, powers of attorney

Finally, there are four tiers to generational wealth building:

- **Tier 1 Unprepared** – you haven't done any thinking or planning about your legacy

- **Tier 2 Insurance Only** – you have life insurance but haven't communicated comprehensively about your wishes to your family.

- **Tier 3 Estate Planned** – you have life insurance, an updated will, and an estate plan.

- **Tier 4 Family Prepared** – you have everything in Tier 3, AND you have and continue to have family meetings to ensure that everybody is educated and knows the plan.

Which tier represents you?

Take ACTION

- Schedule a family meeting (in-person or virtually) to talk about your family's legacy in three areas:
  - **Knowledge:** what is the essential knowledge and wisdom you should pass down to generations in your family?
  - **Tradition / Culture:** what are the traditions specific to your family and cultural heritage that you need to maintain?
  - **Financial:** what is the collective financial wealth of your family – and what is your vision for that wealth?

- If you don't have a will; schedule time with a lawyer to write one (or if that is too expensive, buy a template and fill it out). The point is to put down your final wishes so that your loved ones will not have to guess.

- If you don't have it already, get life insurance and designate one or more beneficiaries.

You have money in the bank – Spend it wisely!

> *"'For I know the plans I have for you,'*
> *declares the Lord, 'plans to prosper you and not*
> *to harm you, plans to give you hope and a future.'"*
>
> (Jeremiah 29:11)

I hope you have experienced a wealth of information and strategies to help you become a better steward of your finances. You can think of everything that I have shared with you as "money in the bank" – you can count on it to work as long as you realize three things:

- **There is a plan** for your money – whether you are making the plan or somebody else is making it for you.

- You need to **work the plan** – choose to take control of the program for your money and then work the plan.

- If you work the plan, **you will win** – your action on the principles and strategies you have learned will bear fruit because they include God's perspective on money and how He wants you to manage it.

You are just at the beginning of your journey.

If you would like to strengthen your plan and make sure you execute it, you need four things: desire, focus, accountability, and consistency. You already have the first one because you signed up for this 21-Day Fast Start – you now need to focus and clarify your goals.

The first way to do this is to read my book (if you haven't already), *The Wealth Cycle*. I go into much deeper detail about the concepts I shared in this series, and reading that detail will help the ideas stick.

The second way to get focused is to pick your top three financial goals and write them out clearly. If you are married, do this with your spouse. Just writing out the goals makes them much more concrete.

If you have read the book and written out your goals, use the book as a reference for the actions you should take to accomplish each goal.

Then do what it says to do.

Made in the USA
Las Vegas, NV
27 November 2024